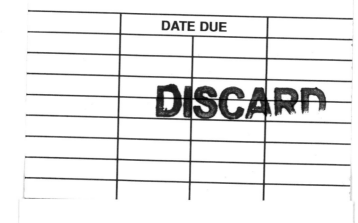

CINCO DE MAYO

HOLIDAY CELEBRATIONS

Kieran Walsh

Rourke
Publishing LLC
Vero Beach, Florida 32964

www.rourkepublishing.com

PHOTO CREDITS: © Oscar C. Williams pages 10, 13; © Associated Press all other photos

Cover: *Girls dressed in traditional Mexican costumes ride on a float during Cinco de Mayo parade in Detroit. Michigan.*

Editor: Frank Sloan

Cover Design by Nicola Stratford

Library of Congress Cataloging-in-Publication Data

Walsh, Kieran.
  Cinco de mayo : holiday celebrations / Kieran Walsh.
      p. cm. — (Holiday celebrations)
Includes index.
  ISBN 1-58952-221-4 (hardcover)
  1. Cinco de Mayo (Mexican holiday)—Juvenile literature. 2.
Mexico—Social life and customs—Juvenile literature. 3. Cinco de Mayo,
Battle of, 1862—Juvenile literature. I. Title: 5 de mayo. II. Title.
III. Holiday celebrations (Vero Beach, Fla.)
  F1233 .W35 2002
  394.26972--dc21
                                                    2002003672

Printed in the USA

CG/CG

TABLE OF CONTENTS

THE FIFTH OF MAY

Cinco de Mayo (SINK oh day MY oh) is Spanish for "The Fifth of May." The fifth of May is the anniversary of a great battle between the French and the Mexicans. The Mexicans won the battle. Every year on the fifth of May Mexican people honor their victory with a celebration known as Cinco de Mayo.

Cinco de Mayo is a national holiday in Mexico.

THE CELEBRATION

Cinco de Mayo is a celebration of Mexican culture, food, and music. Cinco de Mayo is a national holiday in Mexico. Mexicans living in America also celebrate Cinco de Mayo with parties, dancing, and music. More and more people join the fun every year.

Traditional Mexican music draws a crowd at Cinco de Mayo.

PARADES

American cities with a large Mexican population have parades for Cinco de Mayo. San Francisco, Chicago, and Detroit are just a few of the cities that have parades. In the parades are bicycles, dancers, and floats. People wear flowers, Mexican costumes, and wave colorful banners. **Mariachi** bands play traditional Mexican music.

Partygoers are treated to a Mariachi band performance.

FOOD

For Cinco de Mayo, people celebrate with a variety of tasty foods. One traditional Mexican food is **menudo**. Menudo is a soup made from tripe, chili, and spices. Modern favorites include salsa and chips, **burritos**, and **quesadillas**.

Traditional favorites are served at the celebration.

Music and dancing are always part of the celebration.

Children enjoy frozen treats at Cinco de Mayo.

GAMES

On Cinco de Mayo, people enjoy playing Mexican games like **Loteria**, which is similar to Bingo. The **piñata** game is also popular. The piñata is a large paper toy filled with candy. Piñatas are usually made in the shape of an animal such as a donkey. While blindfolded, people hit the piñata with a stick until it breaks open. Then the candy spills out for everyone to eat!

Trying to hit a swinging piñata isn't easy.

MEXICO AND FRANCE

Mexico gained independence from Spain in 1821. Afterward, Mexicans had to borrow money from other nations to build their country. One country Mexico owed a lot of money to was France. The French leader Napoleon decided to claim Mexico for the French empire. Starting at the Gulf of Mexico, French troops began a march toward Mexico City.

French troops advance on the Mexican army in this battle reenactment at Puebla.

PUEBLA

The President of Mexico sent General Ignacio **Zaragosa** and his army to defend Mexico against the French. The French army numbered about 8,000 soldiers. General Zaragosa only had about 4,500 troops. On the morning of May 5, 1862, the French and Mexican armies fought in the town of **Puebla**, Mexico. Although there were more French soldiers, the Mexicans managed to drive back the French.

Girls dressed in their finest pose in front of a statue of General Ignacio Zaragosa.

FIESTA

Fiesta is a Spanish word meaning "celebration." On Friday, May 4, 2001, President George Bush and Mrs. Laura Bush hosted the first Cinco de Mayo Fiesta on the South Lawn of the White House. Attending the fiesta were around 300 Mexican celebrities and performers. President Bush gave a speech at the fiesta announcing "Mi Casa Blanca es su Casa Blanca." In English this means, "My White House is Your White House."

President George Bush and Mrs. Bush greet guests at the Cinco de Mayo celebration at the White House.

THE STATUE IN PUEBLA

In the town of Puebla, Mexico, the battlefield where the French and Mexican troops once fought is now a park. This park includes a war museum. There toy soldiers are used to show how the battle was won. Also, there is a statue of General Zaragosa riding on his horse. This statue is a reminder of the importance of Cinco de Mayo and the courage of the Mexican people.

GLOSSARY

burritos (boor EAT ohz) — a rolled soft tortilla shell stuffed with cheese, sour cream, chicken, or steak

fiesta (fee ES tah) — a Spanish word that means "celebration"

Loteria (loh ter EE ah) — a game similar to Bingo

mariachi (MAHR ee ah chee) — a Mexican street band

menudo (muh NEW doh) — a soup made from tripe, chili, and other spices

piñata (peen YAH tuh) — a paper toy filled with candies

Puebla (pu AY bluh) — the town in Mexico where the Mexicans defeated the French

quesadillas (kay say DEE ahz) — a food made of flat tortillas stuffed with cheese, guacamole, and salsa

Zaragosa (zah rah GO suh) — the general who defeated the French on the fifth of May

INDEX

Further Reading

Schaefer, Lola M. *Cinco de Mayo*. Pebble Books, 2001

Urrutia, Maria Cristina. *Cinco de Mayo: Yesterday and Today*. Groundwood
    Books, 2002

Vazquez, Sarah. *Cinco de Mayo*. Raintree-Steck Vaughn, 1999

Websites To Visit

http://spanish.about.com/library/weekly/aa050100b.htm

http://www.vivacincodemayo.org/history.htm

About The Author

Kieran Walsh is a writer of children's nonfiction books, primarily on historical and
social studies topics. A graduate of Manhattan College, in Riverdale, NY, his degree
is in Communications. Walsh has been involved in the children's book field as editor,
proofreader, and illustrator as well as author.